Introduction

Interpretation of results

More than 83 percent of the CFPB employee population responded to the third annual employee survey conducted by the Consumer Financial Protection Bureau (CFPB) between July 15, 2014 and August 15, 2014.

Bureau leaders use feedback from tools like the annual employee survey to develop strategies to better serve employee needs. Survey results are shared across the organization to encourage leaders to actively seek and respond to opportunities to improve the employee work experience.

The 2014 survey results reveal that the majority of employees identify strongly with the CFPB mission, among other strengths. Of 75 questions included in the survey, employees responded favorably (65 percent or higher agree/satisfied or strongly agree/very satisfied) to 38 items. In the 2014 survey results, 4 items were identified as challenges with percent unfavorable (percent of respondents who disagree/strong disagree or are dissatisfied/very dissatisfied) results greater than 35%.

CFPB continues to develop as an organization and is actively leveraging employee feedback to inform organizational goals and activity. The Bureau has established a robust process to respond to the areas of improvement identified through the survey. CFPB is collaborating with the National Treasury Employees Union (NTEU) to design and implement tailored interventions at all levels of the organization.

How the survey was conducted

The survey was conducted online from July 15, 2014, to August 15, 2014.

Survey items and response choices

See Tables 1 through 16 on the following pages for information on the number and percentage of survey respondents selecting each response scale choice. Tables are organized into content areas representing perceptions of the following:

- My work experience;
- My agency;
- My supervisor;
- Leadership;
- Rewards and recognition: Work unit;
- Rewards and recognition: Agency;
- Diversity and inclusion; and
- Overall satisfaction.

In each content area, the number of respondents (frequencies) and percentage of respondents selecting each response scale choice are provided separately. Tables are presented so that the first table shows the frequency or number of respondents who selected each response scale choice. The first table, therefore, also shows the total number of respondents for each item[1]. The percentage of respondents for each item and response scale choice[2] is shown in the second table.

Description of sample

All 1,372 full time equivalent agency employees on board as of July 1, 2014 were surveyed.

---

[1] Survey respondents were informed that "responses to this survey are voluntary and there is no penalty if you choose not to respond."

[2] Some items included an option for survey respondents to select "Do Not Know" or "No Basis to Judge." These items are noted in Tables 1 to 16. The number of respondents who selected "Do Not Know" or "No Basis to Judge" is not included in calculating percentages.

Number of employees surveyed, number who responded, and representativeness of respondents

Of the 1,372 employees surveyed, 1,145 responded, for an 83.5% response rate. These respondents are representative of the population. Demographic information (percent representation) for survey respondents compared to CFPB population statistics is presented in Tables 17 through 21.

2014 Annual employee survey results for Consumer Financial Protection Bureau all respondents

SURVEYS SENT: 1372

SURVEYS RETURNED: 1145

RESPONSE RATE: 83.5%

TABLE 1:   MY WORK EXPERIENCE—FREQUENCIES

Item Text	Strongly Agree	Agree	Neither	Disagree	Strongly Disagree	Do Not Know	Total
1. I have enough information to do my job well.	226	621	137	136	24	NA	1,144
2. I feel encouraged to come up with new and better ways of doing things.	333	452	162	124	69	NA	1,140
3. My work gives me a feeling of personal accomplishment.	417	470	146	74	31	NA	1,138
4. I like the kind of work I do.	484	495	110	38	8	NA	1,135
5. I have sufficient resources (for example, people, materials, budget) to get my job done.	150	462	160	249	122	0	1,143
6. My workload is reasonable.	123	531	166	209	111	1	1,140

Item Text	Strongly Agree	Agree	Neither	Disagree	Strongly Disagree	Do Not Know	Total
7. I know how my work relates to the agency's goals and priorities.	419	568	73	53	25	1	1,138
8. The work I do is important.	616	426	70	20	10	2	1,142
9. I find it easy to stay fully engaged in my work.	277	544	175	116	31	NA	1,143
10. I get excited when I think about what I could accomplish at work.	353	463	210	87	27	NA	1,140
11. I am given a real opportunity to improve my skills in my organization.	246	459	195	160	76	NA	1,136
12. I can make decisions without first checking with my supervisor.	165	469	196	173	130	9	1,133
13. Employees have a feeling of personal empowerment with respect to work processes.	118	347	256	239	162	17	1,122
14. Supervisors in my work unit support employee development.	318	500	140	93	83	7	1,134
15. My training needs are assessed.	137	425	259	195	104	18	1,120

Item Text	Very Satisfied	Satisfied	Neither	Dis-satisfied	Very Dis-satisfied	Total
16. How satisfied are you with the training you receive for your present job?	141	428	328	179	63	1,139

Item Text	Strongly Agree	Agree	Neither	Disagree	Strongly Disagree	Do Not Know	Total
17. The people I work with cooperate to get the job done.	360	526	118	65	26	NA	1,095
18. I have good friends at work.	346	566	174	40	14	2	1,140
19. Employees in my work unit share job knowledge with each other.	423	576	77	38	26	2	1,140
20. The people in my work unit take on new responsibilities as the need arises.	400	568	101	43	19	13	1,131
21. The people in my work unit look for ways to improve the way we work.	357	566	122	64	23	9	1,132
22. In my work unit, we take steps to ensure the quality of our work.	409	581	92	38	20	4	1,140
23. The people I work with help each other out.	455	538	88	35	23	3	1,139
24. The people in my work unit fix little problems before they become major issues.	275	505	206	84	50	19	1,120
25. My work unit is able to recruit people with the right skills.	215	419	267	130	76	34	1,107
26. The skill level in my work unit has improved in the past year.	257	454	252	81	42	52	1,086

Item Text	Very Good	Good	Fair	Poor	Very Poor	Total
27. How would you rate the overall quality of work done by your work unit?	567	431	113	15	10	1,136

TABLE 2: MY WORK EXPERIENCE—PERCENTAGES

Item Text	Strongly Agree	Agree	Neither	Disagree	Strongly Disagree	Total
1. I have enough information to do my job well.	19.8%	54.3%	12.0%	11.9%	2.1%	100.0%
2. I feel encouraged to come up with new and better ways of doing things.	29.2%	39.6%	14.2%	10.9%	6.1%	100.0%
3. My work gives me a feeling of personal accomplishment.	36.6%	41.3%	12.8%	6.5%	2.7%	100.0%
4. I like the kind of work I do.	42.6%	43.6%	9.7%	3.3%	0.7%	100.0%
5. I have sufficient resources (for example, people, materials, budget) to get my job done.	13.1%	40.4%	14.0%	21.8%	10.7%	100.0%
6. My workload is reasonable.	10.8%	46.6%	14.6%	18.3%	9.7%	100.0%
7. I know how my work relates to the agency's goals and priorities.	36.8%	49.9%	6.4%	4.7%	2.2%	100.0%
8. The work I do is important.	53.9%	37.3%	6.1%	1.8%	0.9%	100.0%
9. I find it easy to stay fully engaged in my work.	24.2%	47.6%	15.3%	10.1%	2.7%	100.0%
10. I get excited when I think about what I could accomplish at work.	31.0%	40.6%	18.4%	7.6%	2.4%	100.0%
11. I am given a real opportunity to improve my skills in my organization.	21.7%	40.4%	17.2%	14.1%	6.7%	100.0%
12. I can make decisions without first checking with my supervisor.	14.6%	41.4%	17.3%	15.3%	11.5%	100.0%
13. Employees have a feeling of personal empowerment with respect to work processes.	10.5%	30.9%	22.8%	21.3%	14.4%	100.0%

Item Text	Strongly Agree	Agree	Neither	Disagree	Strongly Disagree	Total
14. Supervisors in my work unit support employee development.	28.0%	44.1%	12.3%	8.2%	7.3%	100.0%
15. My training needs are assessed.	12.2%	37.9%	23.1%	17.4%	9.3%	100.0%

Item Text	Very Satisfied	Satisfied	Neither	Dis-satisfied	Very Dis-satisfied	Total
16. How satisfied are you with the training you receive for your present job?	12.4%	37.6%	28.8%	15.7%	5.5%	100.0%

Item Text	Strongly Agree	Agree	Neither	Disagree	Strongly Disagree	Total
17. The people I work with cooperate to get the job done.	32.9%	48.0%	10.8%	5.9%	2.4%	100.0%
18. I have good friends at work.	30.4%	49.6%	15.3%	3.5%	1.2%	100.0%
19. Employees in my work unit share job knowledge with each other.	37.1%	50.5%	6.8%	3.3%	2.3%	100.0%
20. The people in my work unit take on new responsibilities as the need arises.	35.4%	50.2%	8.9%	3.8%	1.7%	100.0%
21. The people in my work unit look for ways to improve the way we work.	31.5%	50.0%	10.8%	5.7%	2.0%	100.0%
22. In my work unit, we take steps to ensure the quality of our work.	35.9%	51.0%	8.1%	3.3%	1.8%	100.0%
23. The people I work with help each other out.	39.9%	47.2%	7.7%	3.1%	2.0%	100.0%

Item Text	Strongly Agree	Agree	Neither	Disagree	Strongly Disagree	Total
24. The people in my work unit fix little problems before they become major issues.	24.6%	45.1%	18.4%	7.5%	4.5%	100.0%
25. My work unit is able to recruit people with the right skills.	19.4%	37.9%	24.1%	11.7%	6.9%	100.0%
26. The skill level in my work unit has improved in the past year.	23.7%	41.8%	23.2%	7.5%	3.9%	100.0%

Item Text	Very Good	Good	Fair	Poor	Very Poor	Total
27. How would you rate the overall quality of work done by your work unit?	49.9%	37.9%	9.9%	1.3%	0.9%	100.0%

TABLE 3: MY AGENCY—FREQUENCIES

Item Text	Strongly Agree	Agree	Neither	Disagree	Strongly Disagree	Do Not Know	Total
28. The workforce has the job-relevant knowledge and skills necessary to accomplish organizational goals.	207	586	196	88	55	9	1,132
29. My talents are used well in the workplace.	212	467	187	177	99	1	1,142
30. Physical conditions (for example, noise level, temperature, lighting, cleanliness in the workplace) allow employees to perform their jobs well.	210	479	193	120	117	24	1,119
31. Employees are protected from health and safety hazards on the job.	356	523	144	34	41	43	1,098
32. My organization has prepared employees for potential security threats.	186	486	251	122	52	46	1,097

TABLE 4: MY AGENCY—PERCENTAGES

Item Text	Strongly Agree	Agree	Neither	Disagree	Strongly Disagree	Total
28. The workforce has the job-relevant knowledge and skills necessary to accomplish organizational goals.	18.3%	51.8%	17.3%	7.8%	4.9%	100.0%
29. My talents are used well in the workplace.	18.6%	40.9%	16.4%	15.5%	8.7%	100.0%
30. Physical conditions (for example, noise level, temperature, lighting, cleanliness in the workplace) allow employees to perform their jobs well.	18.8%	42.8%	17.2%	10.7%	10.5%	100.0%
31. Employees are protected from health and safety hazards on the job.	32.4%	47.6%	13.1%	3.1%	3.7%	100.0%
32. My organization has prepared employees for potential security threats.	17.0%	44.3%	22.9%	11.1%	4.7%	100.0%

TABLE 5: MY SUPERVISOR—FREQUENCIES

Item Text	Strongly Agree	Agree	Neither	Disagree	Strongly Disagree	Do Not Know	Total
33. I know what is expected of me on the job.	253	597	151	94	32	NA	1,127
34. My performance appraisal is a fair reflection of my performance.	221	453	192	110	98	67	1,074
35. In my work unit, steps are taken to deal with a poor performer who cannot or will not improve.	75	208	285	188	158	226	914
36. In my work unit, differences in performance are recognized in a meaningful way.	78	200	276	234	195	148	983

Item Text	Strongly Agree	Agree	Neither	Disagree	Strongly Disagree	No Basis to Judge	Total
37. In my most recent performance appraisal, I understood what I had to do to be rated at different performance levels (for example, Fully Successful, Outstanding).	159	367	203	160	159	91	1,048

Item Text	Strongly Agree	Agree	Neither	Disagree	Strongly Disagree	Do Not Know	Total
38. Discussions with my supervisor about my performance are worthwhile.	278	480	178	118	76	15	1,130
39. My supervisor provides me with opportunities to demonstrate my leadership skills.	323	474	148	116	75	9	1,136
40. My supervisor provides me with constructive suggestions to improve my job performance.	281	425	214	124	82	11	1,126
41. My supervisor supports my need to balance work and other life issues.	449	464	133	32	52	8	1,130
42. My supervisor is committed to a workforce representative of all segments of society.	417	402	144	32	44	95	1,039
43. In the last six months, my supervisor has talked with me about my performance.	418	588	73	48	14	NA	1,141
44. My supervisor listens to what I have to say.	500	472	87	55	29	NA	1,143
45. My supervisor treats me with respect.	582	432	69	35	25	NA	1,143
46. I have trust and confidence in my supervisor.	479	361	163	78	54	NA	1,135

Item Text	Very Good	Good	Fair	Poor	Very Poor	Total
47. Overall, how good a job do you feel is being done by your immediate supervisor?	523	338	169	60	42	1,132

TABLE 6: MY SUPERVISOR—PERCENTAGES

Item Text	Strongly Agree	Agree	Neither	Disagree	Strongly Disagree	Total
33. I know what is expected of me on the job.	22.4%	53.0%	13.4%	8.3%	2.8%	100.0%
34. My performance appraisal is a fair reflection of my performance.	20.6%	42.2%	17.9%	10.2%	9.1%	100.0%
35. In my work unit, steps are taken to deal with a poor performer who cannot or will not improve.	8.2%	22.8%	31.2%	20.6%	17.3%	100.0%
36. In my work unit, differences in performance are recognized in a meaningful way.	7.9%	20.3%	28.1%	23.8%	19.8%	100.0%

Item Text	Strongly Agree	Agree	Neither	Disagree	Strongly Disagree	Total
37. In my most recent performance appraisal, I understood what I had to do to be rated at different performance levels (for example, Fully Successful, Outstanding).	15.2%	35.0%	19.4%	15.3%	15.2%	100.0%

Item Text	Strongly Agree	Agree	Neither	Disagree	Strongly Disagree	Total
38. Discussions with my supervisor about my performance are worthwhile.	24.6%	42.5%	15.8%	10.4%	6.7%	100.0%
39. My supervisor provides me with opportunities to demonstrate my leadership skills.	28.4%	41.7%	13.0%	10.2%	6.6%	100.0%

Item Text	Strongly Agree	Agree	Neither	Disagree	Strongly Disagree	Total
40. My supervisor provides me with constructive suggestions to improve my job performance.	25.0%	37.7%	19.0%	11.0%	7.3%	100.0%
41. My supervisor supports my need to balance work and other life issues.	39.7%	41.1%	11.8%	2.8%	4.6%	100.0%
42. My supervisor is committed to a workforce representative of all segments of society.	40.1%	38.7%	13.9%	3.1%	4.2%	100.0%
43. In the last six months, my supervisor has talked with me about my performance.	36.6%	51.5%	6.4%	4.2%	1.2%	100.0%
44. My supervisor listens to what I have to say.	43.7%	41.3%	7.6%	4.8%	2.5%	100.0%
45. My supervisor treats me with respect.	50.9%	37.8%	6.0%	3.1%	2.2%	100.0%
46. I have trust and confidence in my supervisor.	42.2%	31.8%	14.4%	6.9%	4.8%	100.0%

Item Text	Very Good	Good	Fair	Poor	Very Poor	Total
47. Overall, how good a job do you feel is being done by your immediate supervisor?	46.2%	29.9%	14.9%	5.3%	3.7%	100.0%

TABLE 7: LEADERSHIP—FREQUENCIES

Item Text	Strongly Agree	Agree	Neither	Disagree	Strongly Disagree	Do Not Know	Total
48. In my organization, senior leaders generate high levels of motivation and commitment in the workforce.	159	397	255	181	129	22	1,121
49. My organization's senior leaders maintain high standards of honesty and integrity.	256	420	209	104	100	56	1,089

Item Text	Strongly Agree	Agree	Neither	Disagree	Strongly Disagree	Do Not Know	Total
50. Managers communicate the goals and priorities of the organization.	184	535	207	126	85	8	1,137
51. Managers review and evaluate the organization's progress toward meeting its goals and objectives.	166	495	228	96	61	93	1,046
52. Managers promote communication among different work units (for example, about projects, goals, needed resources).	158	469	220	160	106	30	1,113
53. Managers support collaboration across work units to accomplish work objectives.	188	485	220	127	89	31	1,109
54. I have a high level of respect for my organization's senior leaders.	232	430	236	120	107	11	1,125

Item Text	Very Satisfied	Satisfied	Neither	Dis-satisfied	Very Dis-satisfied	Total
55. How satisfied are you with your involvement in decisions that affect your work?	164	406	280	221	72	1,143
56. How satisfied are you with the information you receive from management on what's going on in your organization?	141	423	263	232	83	1,142
57. How satisfied are you with the policies and practices of your senior leaders?	122	388	302	238	88	1,138

TABLE 8: LEADERSHIP—PERCENTAGES

Item Text	Strongly Agree	Agree	Neither	Disagree	Strongly Disagree	Total
48. In my organization, senior leaders generate high levels of motivation and commitment in the workforce.	14.2%	35.4%	22.7%	16.1%	11.5%	100.0%
49. My organization's senior leaders maintain high standards of honesty and integrity.	23.5%	38.6%	19.2%	9.6%	9.2%	100.0%
50. Managers communicate the goals and priorities of the organization.	16.2%	47.1%	18.2%	11.1%	7.5%	100.0%
51. Managers review and evaluate the organization's progress toward meeting its goals and objectives.	15.9%	47.3%	21.8%	9.2%	5.8%	100.0%
52. Managers promote communication among different work units (for example, about projects, goals, needed resources).	14.2%	42.1%	19.8%	14.4%	9.5%	100.0%
53. Managers support collaboration across work units to accomplish work objectives.	17.0%	43.7%	19.8%	11.5%	8.0%	100.0%
54. I have a high level of respect for my organization's senior leaders.	20.6%	38.2%	21.0%	10.7%	9.5%	100.0%

Item Text	Very Satisfied	Satisfied	Neither	Dissatisfied	Very Dissatisfied	Total
55. How satisfied are you with your involvement in decisions that affect your work?	14.3%	35.5%	24.5%	19.3%	6.3%	100.0%
56. How satisfied are you with the information you receive from management on what's going on in your organization?	12.3%	37.0%	23.0%	20.3%	7.3%	100.0%
57. How satisfied are you with the policies and practices of your senior leaders?	10.7%	34.1%	26.5%	20.9%	7.7%	100.0%

TABLE 9: REWARDS AND RECOGNITION: WORK UNIT—FREQUENCIES

Item Text	Strongly Agree	Agree	Neither	Disagree	Strongly Disagree	Do Not Know	Total
58. Promotions in my work unit are based on merit.	121	261	238	152	172	199	944
59. Awards in my work unit depend on how well employees perform their jobs.	112	241	246	127	169	243	895

TABLE 10: REWARDS AND RECOGNITION: WORK UNIT—PERCENTAGES

Item Text	Strongly Agree	Agree	Neither	Disagree	Strongly Disagree	Total
58. Promotions in my work unit are based on merit.	12.8%	27.6%	25.2%	16.1%	18.2%	100.0%
59. Awards in my work unit depend on how well employees perform their jobs.	12.5%	26.9%	27.5%	14.2%	18.9%	100.0%

TABLE 11: REWARDS AND RECOGNITION: AGENCY—FREQUENCIES

Item Text	Strongly Agree	Agree	Neither	Disagree	Strongly Disagree	Do Not Know	Total
60. Employees are recognized for providing high quality products and services.	138	413	226	155	123	87	1,055
61. Creativity and innovation are rewarded.	126	351	273	149	131	112	1,030
62. Pay raises depend on how well employees perform their jobs.	73	191	274	178	221	199	937

Item Text	Very Satisfied	Satisfied	Neither	Dis-satisfied	Very Dis-satisfied	Total
63. How satisfied are you with the recognition you receive for doing a good job?	180	423	281	184	69	1,137
64. How satisfied are you with your opportunity to get a better job in your organization?	121	261	393	223	136	1,134

TABLE 12: REWARDS AND RECOGNITION: AGENCY—PERCENTAGES

Item Text	Strongly Agree	Agree	Neither	Disagree	Strongly Disagree	Total
60. Employees are recognized for providing high quality products and services.	13.1%	39.1%	21.4%	14.7%	11.7%	100.0%
61. Creativity and innovation are rewarded.	12.2%	34.1%	26.5%	14.5%	12.7%	100.0%
62. Pay raises depend on how well employees perform their jobs.	7.8%	20.4%	29.2%	19.0%	23.6%	100.0%

Item Text	Very Satisfied	Satisfied	Neither	Dis-satisfied	Very Dis-satisfied	Total
63. How satisfied are you with the recognition you receive for doing a good job?	15.8%	37.2%	24.7%	16.2%	6.1%	100.0%
64. How satisfied are you with your opportunity to get a better job in your organization?	10.7%	23.0%	34.7%	19.7%	12.0%	100.0%

TABLE 13: DIVERSITY AND INCLUSION—FREQUENCIES

Item Text	Strongly Agree	Agree	Neither	Disagree	Strongly Disagree	Do Not Know	Total
65. Supervisors work well with employees of different backgrounds.	254	497	167	90	65	67	1,073
66. I can disclose a suspected violation of any law, rule or regulation without fear of reprisal.	301	389	174	76	80	122	1,020
67. Differences among individuals (for example, gender, race, national origin, religion, age, cultural background, disability, sexual orientation) are respected and valued.	331	468	155	82	59	47	1,095
68. Advancement opportunities are available for qualified individuals, regardless of gender, race, national origin, religion, age, cultural background, disability, or sexual orientation.	270	362	170	108	100	132	1,010
69. Policies and programs promote diversity in the workplace (for example, recruiting minorities and women, training in awareness of diversity issues, mentoring).	276	423	186	88	79	88	1,052
70. Arbitrary action, personal favoritism and coercion for partisan political purposes are not tolerated.	238	297	198	122	141	144	996
71. Prohibited Personnel Practices (for example, illegally discriminating for or against any employee/applicant, obstructing a person's right to compete for employment, knowingly violating veterans' preference requirements) are not tolerated.	307	348	183	56	77	169	971

TABLE 14: DIVERSITY AND INCLUSION—PERCENTAGES

Item Text	Strongly Agree	Agree	Neither	Disagree	Strongly Disagree	Total
65. Supervisors work well with employees of different backgrounds.	23.7%	46.3%	15.6%	8.4%	6.1%	100.0%
66. I can disclose a suspected violation of any law, rule or regulation without fear of reprisal.	29.5%	38.1%	17.1%	7.5%	7.8%	100.0%
67. Differences among individuals (for example, gender, race, national origin, religion, age, cultural background, disability, sexual orientation) are respected and valued.	30.2%	42.7%	14.2%	7.5%	5.4%	100.0%
68. Advancement opportunities are available for qualified individuals, regardless of gender, race, national origin, religion, age, cultural background, disability, or sexual orientation.	26.7%	35.8%	16.8%	10.7%	9.9%	100.0%
69. Policies and programs promote diversity in the workplace (for example, recruiting minorities and women, training in awareness of diversity issues, mentoring).	26.2%	40.2%	17.7%	8.4%	7.5%	100.0%
70. Arbitrary action, personal favoritism and coercion for partisan political purposes are not tolerated.	23.9%	29.8%	19.9%	12.2%	14.2%	100.0%
71. Prohibited Personnel Practices (for example, illegally discriminating for or against any employee/applicant, obstructing a person's right to compete for employment, knowingly violating veterans' preference requirements) are not tolerated.	31.6%	35.8%	18.8%	5.8%	7.9%	100.0%

TABLE 15: OVERALL SATISFACTION—FREQUENCIES

Item Text	Very Satisfied	Satisfied	Neither	Dis-satisfied	Very Dis-satisfied	Total
72. Considering everything, how satisfied are you with your job?	288	517	180	122	36	1,143
73. Considering everything, how satisfied are you with your pay?	250	436	190	180	88	1,144

Item Text	Very Satisfied	Satisfied	Neither	Dis-satisfied	Very Dis-satisfied	Total
74. Considering everything, how satisfied are you with your organization?	227	507	204	154	50	1,142

Item Text	Strongly Agree	Agree	Neither	Disagree	Strongly Disagree	Total
75. I recommend my organization as a good place to work.	308	434	232	118	50	1,142

TABLE 16: OVERALL SATISFACTION—PERCENTAGES

Item Text	Very Satisfied	Satisfied	Neither	Dis-satisfied	Very Dis-satisfied	Total
72. Considering everything, how satisfied are you with your job?	25.2%	45.2%	15.7%	10.7%	3.1%	100.0%
73. Considering everything, how satisfied are you with your pay?	21.9%	38.1%	16.6%	15.7%	7.7%	100.0%
74. Considering everything, how satisfied are you with your organization?	19.9%	44.4%	17.9%	13.5%	4.4%	100.0%

Item Text	Strongly Agree	Agree	Neither	Disagree	Strongly Disagree	Total
75. I recommend my organization as a good place to work.	27.0%	38.0%	20.3%	10.3%	4.4%	100.0%

Demographics

TABLE 17: SUPERVISORY STATUS

What is your supervisory status?	Population	Respondents
Non-Supervisor	82%	82%
Supervisor and Above	18%	18%

TABLE 18: GENDER

Gender	Population	Respondents
Male	53%	56%
Female	47%	44%

TABLE 19: ARE YOU: HISPANIC OR LATINO

Are you Hispanic or Latino?	Population	Respondents
Yes	6%	7%
No	94%	93%

TABLE 20: RACIAL CATEGORY

Please select the racial category or categories with which you most closely identify:	Population	Respondents
White	68%	72%
Black or African American	18%	16%
Native Hawaiian or other Pacific Islander	0%	0%
Asian	10%	8%
American Indian or Alaska Native	0%	0%
Two or more races	3%	3%

TABLE 21: DIVISION

Division	Population	Respondents
Office of the Director	2%	2%
Operations	29%	31%
Consumer Education and Engagement	5%	5%
Research, Markets, and Regulations	10%	10%
Supervision, Enforcement, Fair Lending, and Equal Opportunity	46%	44%
External Affairs	3%	3%
Legal Division	4%	5%
Other Programs	2%	0%